No One Saw

Ordinary Things
Through the Eyes of an Artist

by Bob Raczka

The Millbrook Press   Brookfield, Connecticut

Published by The Millbrook Press, Inc.
2 Old New Milford Road, Brookfield, Connecticut 06804
www.millbrookpress.com

Printed in the United States of America
Book design by Tania Garcia
Art research by Pam Szen

Library Edition: 5 4 3 2 1
Paperback: 5 4 3 2 1

Library of Congress Cataloging-in-Publication Data

Raczka, Bob.
No one saw— / by Bob Raczka.
    p. cm.
ISBN 0-7613-2370-8 (lib. bdg.)   0-7613-1648-5 (pbk.)
1. Painting, Modern—19th century—Juvenile literature. 2. Painting,
Modern—20th century—Juvenile literature. [1. Painting, Modern—19th
century. 2. Painting, Modern—20th century. 3. Art appreciation.] I. Title.

ND189 .R33 2002
759.06—dc21   2001030006

To Amy, who saw something
in me that no one else did.

No one saw
flowers
like
Georgia
O'Keeffe.

No one saw
trains like *René Magritte.*

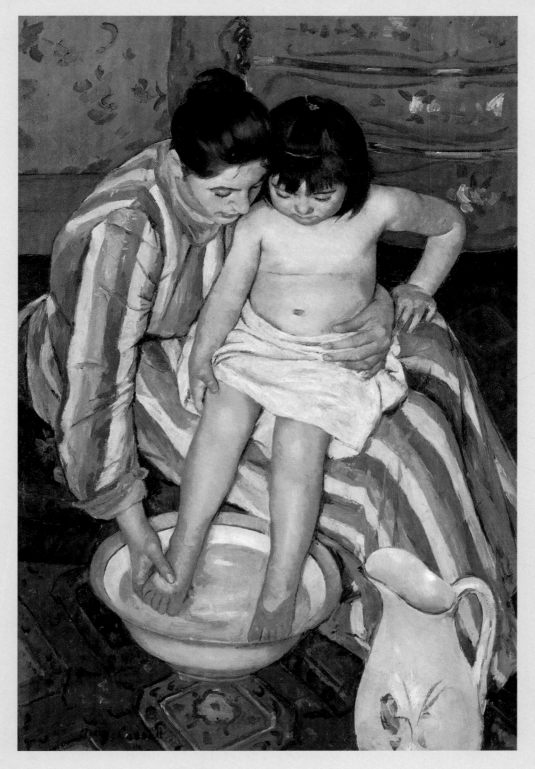

No one saw
mothers like *Mary Cassatt*.

No one saw
Sunday
like
Georges
Seurat.

No one saw
stars
like
Vincent
van Gogh

No one saw
people like *Joan Miró.*

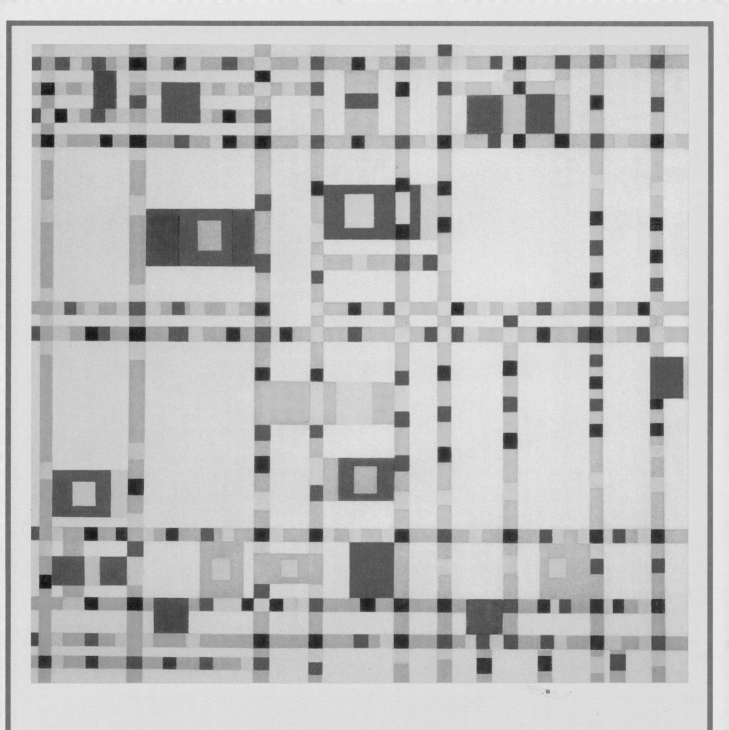

No one saw
squares like *Piet Mondrian.*

No one saw
apples
like
Paul Cézanne.

No one saw
music like *Marc Chagall.*

No one saw
soup like *Andy Warhol.*

No one saw
hay
like
*Claude
Monet.*

No one saw
fish
like
Paul Klee.

No one saw
dancers like *Edgar Degas.*

No one saw
children like *Pierre Renoir.*

23

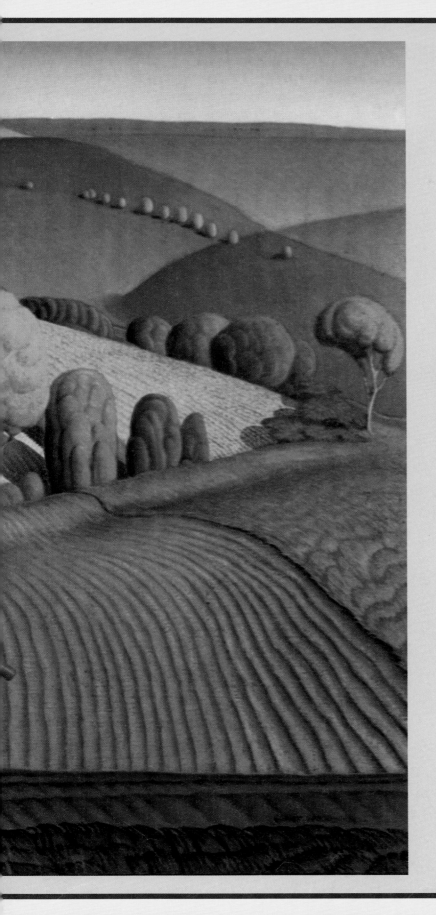

No one saw
*fields and
farms*
like
Grant Wood.

No one saw
cities like *Kandinsky* could.

Artists express their own point of view. And nobody sees the world like *you.*

List of Paintings

Two Calla Lilies on Pink (1928), Georgia O'Keeffe

Time Transfixed (1938), René Magritte

The Child's Bath (c. 1893), Mary Cassatt

A Sunday Afternoon on La Grand Jette (1884–86), Georges Seurat

The Starry Night (June 1889), Vincent van Gogh

Femmes et Oiseau dans la Nuit (1944), Joan Miró

Broadway Boogie-Woogie (1942), Piet Mondrian

The Basket of Apples (c. 1895), Paul Cézanne

Green Violinist (1923–24), Mark Chagall

One Hundred Cans (1962), Andy Warhol

Haystacks at Chaillay (1865), Claude Monet

Fish Magic (1925), Paul Klee

The Star (c. 1879–81), Edgar Degas

Acrobats at the Cirque Fernando (1879), Pierre Renoir

Fall Plowing (1931), Grant Wood

Zuboff Square (1916), Wassily Kandinsky

Biographical Notes

Mary Cassatt (kuh SAT) (1844-1926). Mary was an American painter who lived most of her life in France. In the 1870s, she began experimenting with the bright colors and loose brushstrokes of the *impressionists*. Though she was never a mother herself, Mary is best known for her paintings of mothers and their children.

Paul Cézanne (say ZAHN) (1839-1906). Paul was a French artist who, for the most part, taught himself how to paint. He learned quite a bit by copying masterpieces at the Louvre Museum in Paris, France. Although he worked alongside the *impressionists*, Paul was more interested in the true colors of objects than they were.

Marc Chagall (shah GAHL) (1887-1985). Marc was a Russian artist whose work includes many childhood memories. He didn't care if the sizes of things in his paintings were unrealistic, and he often painted animals, musicians, and lovers floating in the air. Because of this, Marc's style is related to *surrealism*, which means beyond reality.

Edgar Degas (duh GAH) (1834-1917). Edgar was a French painter and a member of the *impressionist* movement. He took great care in drawing his figures, as well as in composing his paintings. Edgar often painted his subjects from unusual angles. He is best known for his scenes of women dancing, shopping, and bathing.

Wassily Kandinsky (VAS uh lee kan DIHN skee) (1866-1944). Wassily was a Russian artist who said painting is like music—it's a way to express yourself without having to tell a story. His early style was quite free and colorful, but it later became geometric and abstract. Wassily is considered to be the father of *abstract* painting, which has no identifiable subject.

Paul Klee (klay) (1879-1940). Paul was a Swiss painter, one of the most inventive in all of modern art. Paul was considered a master of color, even though many of his works seem childlike in their simplicity. Unlike most painters, Paul liked to "work small." He was a great teacher as well, sharing his ideas at the Bauhaus school in Germany during the 1920s.

René Magritte (ma GREET) (1898-1967). René was a Belgian painter who studied art in Brussels. In 1922 he began painting in a style called *surrealism*. By combining things in unusual ways, René created many strange and dreamlike paintings. His particular style is also called *magic realism*.

Joan Miró (hoh AHN mee ROH) (1893-1983). Joan was a Spanish artist who developed a very personal and *abstract* style. His paintings are full of odd shapes that suggest people, animals, and strange, unrecognizable creatures. Joan also worked in ceramics and sculpture.

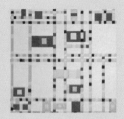

Piet Mondrian (peet MAWN dree ahn) (1872-1944). Piet was a Dutch painter who became famous for a stark, geometric style he called *neoplasticism*. Many of his works feature squares and rectangles painted in the primary colors of red, blue, and yellow. Piet's paintings are also very smooth, with no brushstrokes to be seen.

Claude Monet (moh NAY) (1840-1926). Claude was a French painter who became a leader of the *impressionist* movement. He was very interested in outdoor light. Claude often painted the same subject, such as a haystack, at several different times of day or during different seasons, to show how different light changes the way things look.

Georgia O'Keeffe (1887-1986). Georgia was an American painter who knew she wanted to be an artist when she was just a girl. She began painting large flowers, when she lived in New York, to help pass the long winters there. Georgia later moved to New Mexico, where she painted until her eyes failed her at the age of 85.

Pierre Auguste Renoir (oh GOOST ruh NWAHR) (1841-1919). Pierre was a French *impressionist* who started out painting on porcelain, window shades, and fans. He preferred painting people to landscapes, and he often painted his own wife and children. As Pierre got older, he suffered from arthritis and had to learn to paint with brushes tied to his hands.

Georges Seurat (zharwrzh suh RAH) (1859-1891). Georges was a French artist who explored many formulas for painting. In 1885 and 1886, he and his friend Paul Signac invented *pointillism*, a style of painting using dots of color placed side by side. Seen from a distance, these color dots blend to form new colors, as well as the shapes in his paintings.

Vincent van Gogh (van GOH) (1853–1890). Vincent was a Dutch painter whose early works were very dark in color. But in 1888 he moved to Arles in southern France, where the bright sunlight and the beautiful landscape inspired him to use the brilliant colors that have become his signature. Sadly, Vincent only sold one painting during his lifetime.

Andy Warhol (WAWR hawl) (1930?–1987). Andy is known as an American painter, although his most famous works weren't painted at all. He created them using a mechanical process called silk-screen printing. By simplifying, enlarging, and repeating images of everyday objects and famous people, Andy became a leader of the *pop art* movement in the 1960s.

Grant Wood (1891–1942). Grant was an American *regionalist* painter who believed artists should stay near their homes and paint from personal experience. Most of his paintings feature the people and the farmland of Iowa. Contrary to popular belief, his most famous painting, *American Gothic*, shows a farmer and his daughter — not his wife.

Photo Credits

Cover picture courtesy of SuperStock (*The Starry Night*, Vincent van Gogh, Dutch, 1853–1890. Oil on canvas, 1889, 72 x 92 cm.)

Pictures courtesy of San Diego Museum of Art (Museum purchase): pp. 1 (detail from *Haystacks at Chailly*), 18–19 (*Haystacks at Chailly*, Claude Monet, French, 1840-1926. Oil on canvas, 1865, 11-7/8 x 23-3/4 in.); The Art Institute of Chicago: pp. 2 (detail from *The Basket of Apples*, Paul Cézanne, French, 1839-1906. Oil on canvas c. 1895, 65 x 80 cm. Helen Birch Bartlett Memorial Collection, 1926.252), 6 (*Time Transfixed*, René Magritte, Belgian, 1898-1967. Oil on canvas, 1938, 147 x 98.7 cm. Joseph Winterbotham Collection, 1970.426, © 2001 C. Hersovici, Brussels/Artists Rights Society (ARS), New York), 7 (*The Child's Bath*, Mary Cassatt, American, 1844-1926. Oil on canvas, 1893, 39 1/2 x 26. Robert A. Waller Fund, 1910.2), 8-9 (*A Sunday on La Grande Jatte*, Georges Seurat, French, 1859-1891. Oil on canvas, 1884, 1884-1886, 207.6 x 308 cm. Helen Birch Bartlett Memorial Collection, 1926.224), 14-15 (*The Basket of Apples*, Paul Cézanne, French, 1839-1906. Oil on canvas c. 1895, 65 x 80 cm. Helen Birch Bartlett Memorial Collection, 1926.252), 22 (*The Star*, Edgar Hilaire Germain Degas, French 1834-1917. Pastel on cream wove paper, edge mounted on board, 1879-1881, 73.3 x 57.4 cm. Bequest of Mrs. Diego Suarez, 1980.414), 23 (*Acrobats at the Cirque Fernando*, Pierre Auguste Renoir, French, 1841-1919. Oil on canvas, 1879, 131.5 x 99.5 cm. Potter Palmer Collection, 1922.440); Philadelphia Museum of Art: pp. 4-5 (*Two Calla Lilies on Pink*, Georgia O'Keeffe, American, 1887-1986. Oil on canvas, 1928, 40 x 30. Bequest of Georgia O'Keeffe for the Alfred Stieglitz Collection, 1987-70-4, © 2001 The Georgia O'Keeffe Foundation/Artists Rights Society (ARS), New York), p. 3 (detail from *Fish Magic*) 20-21 (*Fish Magic*, Paul Klee, Swiss, 1879-1940. Oil on canvas mounted on board, 1925, 30 3/8 x 38. The Louise and Walter Arensberg Collection, 50-134-112, © 2001 Artist's Rights Society (ARS), New York/VG Bild-Kunst, Bonn); SuperStock: pp. 10-11 (*The Starry Night*, Vincent van Gogh, Dutch, 1853-1890. Oil on canvas, 1889, 72 x 92 cm.), 13 (*Broadway Boogie Woogie*, Piet Mondrian, Dutch, 1872-1944. Oil on canvas, 1942, 50 x 50, © 2001 Artist's Rights Society (ARS), New York/Beeldrecht, Amsterdam), 26 (*Zuboff Square*, Wassily Kandinsky, Russian, 1866-1944. Tretiakov Gallery, Moscow, Russia, © 2001 Artist's Rights Society (ARS), New York/ADAGP, Paris); Yale University Art Gallery: p. 12 (*Femmes et oiseau dans la nuit*, Joan Miró, Spanish, 1893-1983. Oil on burlap, 1944, 44 x 33.6 cm. Gift of Kay Sage Tanguy, 1963.43.1, © 2001 Artist's Rights Society (ARS), New York/ADAGP, Paris); Solomon R. Guggenheim Museum, New York: p. 16 (*Green Violinist (Violoniste)*, Marc Chagall. Oil on canvas, 1923-24, 198 x 108.6 cm. Gift of Solomon R. Guggenheim, 1937. 37.446. Photograph by David Heald © The Solomon R. Guggenheim Foundation, New York © 2001 Artist's Rights Society (ARS), New York/ADAGP, Paris); © 2001 The Andy Warhol Foundation for the Visual Arts/ARS/Art Resource, NY: p. 17 (*One Hundred Cans*, Andy Warhol. Oil on canvas, 1962, 72 x 52); John Deere Art Collection, Moline, Illinois: pp. 24-25 (*Fall Plowing*, Grant Wood. Oil on canvas, 1931, 29 1/4 x 39 1/4); p. 27 drawing by Lluvia Meyreles, age 4 1/2.